THE YEAR AWAKENING

WOOD DRAGON 2024

ANDREW LAYCOCK

CONTENTS

Introduction   1

A Brief Overview of Chinese Astrology   3

The Chinese Zodiac   5

The Five Elements   12

Overview of The Wood Dragon   15

1964. The Last Wood Dragon Year   18

Dragon Years   23

What to Expect in 2024   27

12 Predictions for 2024   38

2024. What It Means For Us   41

Feng Shui Tips For The Year Of The Wood Dragon   56

Final Thoughts   59

Chinese New Year Dates   60

About The Author   64

INTRODUCTION

2024, the year of the Wood Dragon, is a year that will redefine success. It is a year where obsessions with the latest gadgets, the most expensive cars, and how much money we have in our bank accounts will start to diminish, to be replaced with seeing the value in simple pleasures: community, the planet, the joy gained from being at one with the Earth and those we share it with.

The Wood Dragon's arrival is timely in a world where many people seem to be focused on what they have and what they can get, rather than what they can give. It provides us with a reality check and asks us to ditch the culture of accumulating things and shift towards building genuine connections. It's not just about what's on our wishlist; it's about considering what others need on theirs, not just understanding what our sense of purpose is, but helping others discover and realise their dreams as well.

2024 is a year that we will have the chance to say goodbye to the constant pursuit of material wealth and hello to measuring success by the quality of our relationships, our sense of purpose, and our positive impact on the world. The Wood Dragon reminds us that true happiness isn't found in bank accounts or closets bursting with clothes; it's thriving in the warmth of communities and meaningful connections with those who share similar passions and interests. 2024 is the year of awakening, and invites us to open our eyes to the endless possibilities that unfold when our collective hearts beat for others, not only ourselves. Whether we accept the Wood Dragon's invitation or not, as always, is down to us.

A BRIEF OVERVIEW OF CHINESE ASTROLOGY

Chinese astrology is based on a 12-year cycle, where each year is associated with a specific animal zodiac sign. Individually these animals are like personality influencers, shaping how we tick, who we get along with, and even our destiny. Collectively, the energy from each animal comes together to influence worldwide events. While the future will always remain unpredictable due to the various factors that influence events, by studying Chinese astrology we can anticipate the themes which are likely to characterise the year ahead.

Chinese astrology is based around the lunar year, distinguishing it from Western astrology, which relies on the solar year. The Chinese lunar calendar is a lunisolar system incorporating the moon's phases and the solar year. As each moon phase lasts 29 to 30 days, some Chinese years have twelve lunar months and others thirteen. Each Chinese year starts on a slightly different date, between the 21st of January and the 20th of February, and occurs on the first new moon that appears between these dates. The Chinese New Year signifies the end of winter and the beginning of spring. In 2024, the new Chinese year, the year of the Wood Dragon, begins on the 10th of February and lasts until the 28th of January 2025.

In addition to the moon phases and the twelve zodiac animals, there is one more factor that influences each year, which is the five elements. The five elements; Wood, Fire, Earth, Metal, and Water are associated with the Chinese cosmological concept of Wu Xing, which represents the dynamic interplay and relationships between different forces in the natural world. The cyclical interaction of these elements is thought to contribute to the ebb and flow of energy, shaping the unique qualities of each year. They play a crucial role in shaping the characteristics and dynamics of each Chinese zodiac year. 2024 is represented by the Dragon, the fifth animal in the zodiac and Wood, the first element in the cycle of five elements.

THE CHINESE ZODIAC

Before we look specifically at the Wood Dragon year, and how it is likely to shape our world, it is useful for us to have a brief overview of the characteristics of each zodiac animal in the context of our own lives. This understanding will help us each navigate the year of the Wood Dragon to the best of our ability, knowing what will help us, what may hinder us, and what we can do to overcome any challenges or obstacles that the year may throw our way.

THE RAT

The first animal in the zodiac is the rat. If you are a rat you are likely to be quick-witted, resourceful, adaptable, charming and sociable. Rats are great problem solvers who can see and seize opportunities other animals may ignore. Your downfall is that you can be seen as cunning and opportunistic and, because of this, can be judged more harshly than you deserve. Those born in the year of the rat were born in 1924, 1936, 1948, 1960, 1972, 1984, 1996, 2008 and 2020*

THE OX

The second animal in the zodiac is the ox. If you were born in the year of the ox you are often diligent, honest and reliable. When given a task, you approach it methodically and will not stop until the job is done. You are hardworking, disciplined and strong-willed. Your downfall is that you can be perceived as stubborn and unwilling to look at alternative ways of working, and this can sometimes lead you to taking longer over a job than is strictly necessary. Birth years for the ox are 1925, 1937, 1949, 1961, 1973, 1985, 1997, 2009 and 2021*

THE TIGER

The tiger, the third animal in the zodiac, is brave, competitive, confident and charismatic. Tigers can be ambitious, and when doing a task or action you feel will benefit you, you throw yourself into and commit to it wholeheartedly with a large degree of passion. One of the downfalls of the tiger is impulsiveness and you can commit to actions without thinking things through. This can cause you problems, because when things are not going your way you cannot always be relied upon and can be seen as being unpredictable, alarming those around you. Those born in the year of the tiger were born in 1926, 1938, 1950, 1962, 1974, 1986, 1998, 2010 and 2022*

THE RABBIT

The rabbit is a gentle, quiet, compassionate creature. Your strength is that you are diplomatic, tactful and perceptive. The rabbit can often be called upon in times of trouble, and you always seem to know exactly the right thing to say in difficult situations. This desire to say or do the right thing sometimes means you are considered overly cautious or reserved, and people wonder if what they are hearing is what you think, or what you think they want to hear. The rabbit birth years are 1927, 1939, 1951, 1963, 1975, 1987, 1999, 2011 and 2023*

THE DRAGON

The dragon is charismatic, ambitious and enthusiastic. You are natural leaders who can attract large groups of followers with ease and encourage people to do what you want. You are also adaptable and innovative, and able to see solutions to problems that confound others. As a dragon you are so sure of yourself and your abilities that you can be perceived as arrogant if you are not careful. The dragon years are 1928, 1940, 1952, 1964, 1976, 1988, 2000, 2012 and 2024*.

THE SNAKE

Those born in the year of the snake can be wise, charming and seductive. You have no difficulty making decisions and can easily back up your choices with facts. You are excellent at encouraging people to follow a certain course of action as it is difficult to argue against the detailed rationale you provide. You can have a tendency, though, to keep your own counsel and this can lead to you being perceived as secretive. Those born in the year of the snake were born in 1929, 1941, 1953, 1965, 1977, 1989, 2001 and 2013*

THE HORSE

The horse is an energetic, warm-hearted creature with a big spirit and a sense of adventure. You put vast amounts of energy into whatever you want to do, and your infectious sense of adventure leads others to follow your lead. If things do not go your way, though, the horse can be impatient and force change to happen by making decisions without thinking through the impact of their actions on other people. The year of the horse appeared in 1930, 1942, 1954, 1966, 1978, 1990, 2002 and 2014*.

THE GOAT

The goat is the eighth animal in the zodiac and is creative, compassionate and artistic. A lover of the arts, goats value simple pleasure and can see beauty in most things. Because you care so much about your friends and colleagues you can have a tendency to worry, which leads to periods of indecision as you try to work out what you can do for the best, and which will not upset anyone else. The year of the goat arrived in 1931, 1943, 1955, 1967, 1979, 1991, 2003, and 2015*.

THE MONKEY

Those born in the year of the monkey can be witty, intelligent, ambitious and mischievous. You are quick learners who can turn your hands to most things and are resourceful at finding alternative routes through life if the hand you have been dealt does not go your way. The monkey's ability to make lemonade out of lemons can mean that others envy you and believe that you must be stepping on other people's toes to get ahead. The birth year for monkeys is 1932, 1944, 1956, 1968, 1980, 1992, 2004 and 2016*.

THE ROOSTER

The tenth animal in the zodiac is the rooster, and those born under this sign are confident and flamboyant. Whatever is happening in your life you always think it is important to put on a show. Although this leads some to assume that you are all show and no substance, they couldn't be more wrong. You are prepared to work hard to make the best of any situation. The rooster's downfall is that you can be seen as arrogant and overcritical if you feel that someone else is not giving one hundred percent. Rooster birth years are 1933, 1945, 1957, 1969, 1981, 1993, 2005 and 2017*.

THE DOG

Those born under the year of the dog are loyal, honest, kind and cautious. You have an inflated sense of responsibility and work hard not to let anyone down, even if what you are doing comes at great personal sacrifice to yourself. You are reliable and protective and are a good friend when needed. Your downfall is that you can take a pessimistic view of life and never feel good enough. The year of the dog fell in 1934, 1946, 1958, 1970, 1982, 1994, 2006 and 2018*.

THE BOAR

The final animal in the Chinese zodiac is the boar. The boar is well-grounded, solid and dependable. What you see is what you get with the boar. You do not pretend to be anything other than what you are. Your downfall is that you may love life's pleasures a little too much and overindulge, and you can also be too naive and overly trusting. Boars were born in 1935, 1947, 1959, 1971, 1983, 1995, 2007, and 2019*.

*Because the Chinese Zodiac follows the lunar year, those born between January 1st and February 21st should look at the table at the back of this book for the specific date on which the new year fell in their birth year. If the Chinese New Year occurred after the date of their birth, their birth year falls in the year before. Someone born on the 9th February 2024 for example, will be born under the Year of the Rabbit, not the Year of the Dragon.

THE FIVE ELEMENTS

The Chinese zodiac isn't just about the twelve animal signs, it also has the five elements that shape the ebb and flow of energy in the natural world. Each element appears in each animal sign once, meaning that each combination of animal and element appears once every sixty years. Let's now look at how the elements can shape each year.

WOOD

Wood is the first element and corresponds with spring and new beginnings. It symbolises vitality and expansion and represents the energy of growth, renewal and ambition. In the Chinese zodiac, wood years are associated with new beginnings, fresh perspectives, innovation, planning and youth.

FIRE

The second element in the cycle of elements is fire, which corresponds with the height of summer. Fire is the element associated with passion and transformation. In the Chinese zodiac, fire years are marked by intense action and dynamism, when sparks ignite into flames.

EARTH

The third element is earth, which brings stability and a nurturing presence. In the cycle of life it is like middle age. Earth marks the transition points between summer and autumn, and winter and spring. Earth years are often calming and associated with security, practicality and making what is already in place stronger.

METAL

Metal represents strength, precision and clarity. As the fourth element, it is linked to autumn and is associated with resilience, preparation and determination. In the Chinese zodiac, metal years emphasise discipline, order and accomplishment.

WATER

The final element is water. Water embodies wisdom, adaptability and the natural end to a cycle. It is closely linked to winter and death. Water years emphasise the gaining of knowledge, the utilisation of that knowledge for good, and achievement. It also highlights the power of patience and resilience in our growth as we end the cycle through the five elements a different person, or in another place, than when and where we started.

OVERVIEW OF THE WOOD DRAGON

2024 is the year of the Wood Dragon, an animal that last appeared in 1964 and will not reappear again until 2084. To understand how the year will unfold, we can study the dragon's characteristics and the attributes of the element wood to see how they work together. To gain an insight into how we can best approach the year ahead, we use this knowledge in tandem with our own individual signs. To begin to understand the key themes that will define 2024, we can study the combination of the characteristic of the dragon and the wood element in the context of what has been happening in the world over the last few years. Let us now delve deeper into the Year of the Wood Dragon and see what it will mean to us and the world.

The Wood Dragon is a dynamic force for good, blending the natural leadership qualities of the dragon with the nurturing essence of the wood element. This combination brings forth a year marked by innovation, adaptability, and a commitment to growth for the good of everyone. Wood Dragons are infused with a nurturing and compassionate demeanour. Whatever the Wood Dragon does, it does with the best of intentions, and actions are likely to support the growth of many, not a few. Wood Dragons' caring nature extends beyond their circle and encompasses a broader concern for the welfare of the community and the world.

The Wood Dragon embodies a visionary spirit driven by ambitious goals and a deep-seated desire for growth on both a personal level and in society as a whole. Like a young person taking a gap year with friends to travel and see the world and with it find their purpose, the Wood Dragon can envisage possibilities and inspire others to join them on the journey to where they need to go. This means that not only will individuals have a renewed desire to set and achieve goals this year, and which may take them in a completely different direction to where they have previously been heading, but society as a whole may pause to reflect on the trajectory that they are on, and decide that the world may benefit from a change of direction and a reset.

Innovation and growth are inherent to the Wood Dragon's character. Fuelled by a desire for progress, the Wood Dragon is often drawn to new ideas, technologies, and ways of thinking. Expect a year of technological advancements, linked to initiatives that are good for the planet. New businesses will appear, almost as if overnight, and we can expect many of them to follow a partnership, employee owned or cooperative model. The Wood Dragon is a catalyst for change, able to seek opportunities for personal and collective advancement, and so rather than focus on maximising profits for shareholders there will be much more of a focus on development within communities.

Of course, new ideas and initiatives need to be developed, promoted and gain traction and momentum if they are to be widely used and realise their benefits. The Wood Dragon has a magnetic charm that draws people towards it, and persuades them to step off their standard, well-trodden path and follow them towards a different destination. Their influential nature stems from confidence, intelligence, and an ability to connect with others. This charisma positions them as natural leaders, capable of inspiring and mobilising those around them to achieve something worthwhile. We can expect young people to be heavily involved in social and community movements, leading and mobilising large groups of people to create something of lasting benefit to future generations.

The Wood Dragon often engages in community-building activities, seeking to create positive change and contribute to the greater good. Their sociable nature facilitates collaboration, making them effective contributors to collective endeavours. Community and social partnerships will be pivotal in bringing together individuals, organisations and institutions to address shared goals, tackle challenges, and create positive change. Prevalent themes likely to be the focus this year range from poverty and homelessness to climate change, education and healthcare. Combining resources and expertise between local businesses and non-profit organisations will lead to job creation, skill development programs, and increased access to economic opportunities, ultimately strengthening local economies. Whilst there may not be true levelling up across and within nations, local initiatives will play a part in helping to level up the fortunes of households within communities. These partnerships can develop comprehensive solutions that have a lasting impact on the well-being, and equality within smaller communities.

1964. THE LAST WOOD DRAGON YEAR

To gain more understanding of the themes that will be in evidence as we move through 2024, it is useful to go back to the last time we saw the Wood Dragon, in 1964. That was the last year of awakening as the world found itself at the crossroads of a major cultural shift, politically, socially, technologically and in the arts. Let us look at some of the key events that happened in 1964.

CIVIL RIGHTS MOVEMENT IN THE USA

One of the most consequential events of 1964 was the passage of the Civil Rights Act in the USA. Signed into law on July 2, this landmark legislation aimed to dismantle segregation and end discrimination based on race, colour, religion, sex, or national origin. The act paved the way for the desegregation of public spaces and institutions, altering the legal landscape of racial equality in America.

1964 represented a critical period in the Civil Rights Movement, where legislative victories, grassroots activism, and the leadership of key figures converged to bring about significant change. It marked a turning point in American history, challenging the nation to confront its legacy of discrimination and inspiring future generations to continue the fight for justice and equality.

THE SECOND VATICAN COUNCIL

The Second Vatican Council, which took place from 1962 to 1965, was a significant event in the modern history of the Catholic Church. In 1964, the Council made important decisions that marked a turning point for the Church. One major focus was on reforming the liturgy, the Church's worship practices. Approved in 1964, it aimed to make worship more accessible by allowing everyday languages in the Mass, encouraging greater participation from the laity, and simplifying rituals. These changes were a departure from longstanding traditions intended to deepen the spiritual engagement of the faithful.

Another critical aspect of the Council's work in 1964 was its commitment to ecumenism and interfaith dialogue. It emphasised the Church's desire for unity among Christian denominations and promoted collaboration and understanding with other faiths. This marked a progressive and inclusive shift, recognising the importance of fostering harmony and cooperation on a global scale. It emphasised the Church's responsibility to engage with and respond to the changing social, cultural, and political landscape and highlighted the need for the Church to be relevant and adaptable.

ANTI-APARTHEID MOVEMENT IN SOUTH AFRICA

The term "apartheid" referred to the institutionalised system of racial segregation and discrimination enforced by the South African government. In 1964, this discriminatory regime was at its height, with laws and policies that systematically oppressed and marginalised the majority black population. The realisation of the inherent injustice embedded in apartheid sparked a global awakening to the moral imperative of dismantling this system.

The year 1964 saw the conclusion of the Rivonia Trial, a watershed moment in the Anti-Apartheid Movement. Nelson Mandela and other anti-apartheid leaders faced charges of sabotage and other offences for their role in opposing the apartheid regime. Mandela's impassioned speech during the trial captured the attention of the world, bringing the brutality of apartheid to the forefront of international consciousness.

The harsh sentences handed down to Mandela and his co-accused intensified global outrage and sparked widespread protests. The trial became a focal point for the Anti-Apartheid Movement, galvanising international solidarity and awakening a sense of urgency to challenge the entrenched system of racial injustice.

The cultural boycott against South Africa gained momentum in 1964, with artists, musicians, and intellectuals around the world refusing to perform or engage with the apartheid regime. This cultural awakening demonstrated the power of nonviolent resistance and the importance of global solidarity in the fight against injustice. Artists such as Miriam Makeba and Hugh Masekela used their platforms to raise awareness about the realities of apartheid, contributing to a growing global consciousness.

MAKE LOVE NOT WAR

The statement "Make love, not war" emerged as a powerful mantra during the mid-1960s, particularly associated with the anti-Vietnam War protests. Rooted in widespread social and political upheaval, the slogan encapsulates a rejection of violence and militarism in favour of peace, unity, and love. It reflects a sentiment that emphasises the transformative power of love and human connection to resolve conflicts and promote harmony. The phrase has endured as a timeless call for peaceful coexistence, advocating for diplomacy, empathy, and compassion in addressing global issues.

TECHNOLOGICAL ADVANCEMENTS

1964 was marked by several events that represented significant advancements in the technology field. Many of these innovations, whilst not having immediate significance, paved the way for many of the technologies that we take for granted today.

In April 1964, IBM introduced a family of mainframe computers, a groundbreaking development marking the transition from specialised, incompatible computer models to a compatible family of machines. This became highly influential in the computing industry and played a crucial role in the standardisation and modernisation of computer systems.

Likewise, the development of the Basic Combined Programming Language (BCPL) by Martin Richards at the University of Cambridge in 1964 was a significant step in the evolution of programming languages. BCPL laid the groundwork for subsequent languages and contributed to the ongoing awakening in software development methodologies and language design. Also in 1964 the concept of packet switching, a key element in the development of the ARPANET, the precursor to the internet, was proposed by Paul Baran. This conceptual work laid the foundation for creating a decentralised, robust communication network. Although the internet seems a relatively recent invention, and one we all take for granted today, the idea of packet switching created in 1964 was a crucial step in awakening the information age and the eventual development of the internet.

BEATLEMANIA

The Beatles, comprised of John Lennon, Paul McCartney, George Harrison, and Ringo Starr, burst onto the international music scene in early 1964. Their infectious energy, catchy melodies, and distinctive sound resonated with audiences, sparking unprecedented fan hysteria.

Beatlemania transcended music, becoming a cultural phenomenon influencing fashion, hair trends, and even language. The "mop-top" hairstyle sported by The Beatles became a symbol of rebellion and a distinctive marker of the era. The band's witty interviews and irreverent humour also endeared them to fans, contributing to their iconic status and cultural impact.

Beyond the cultural phenomenon, Beatlemania marked a musical awakening. The Beatles' innovative approach to songwriting and recording techniques expanded the boundaries of popular music. Their experimentation with studio production, use of unconventional instruments, and incorporation of diverse musical styles set the stage for the evolution of rock and pop music in the years to come. The Beatles' influence on the music industry was not just about their popularity; it was about their lasting impact on the artistry and creativity of popular music to this day.

DRAGON YEARS

Before we move onto the key themes and events that we are likely to encounter and experience in 2024, it is useful to understand just some of the events that have happened in the last four dragon years since we last met the Wood Dragon. Whilst not having the exact characteristics of the Wood Dragon, all dragon years share similarities. Innovation, change for the greater good, movements and adaptability are often in evidence when the dragon arrives on the world stage.

1976. FIRE DRAGON

In Soweto, thousands of students protested against the government's policy of compulsory education in Afrikaans, the language associated with the oppressors. The brutal response from the authorities and the violent crackdown on the peaceful protests brought international attention to the injustices of apartheid, sparking a renewed sense of resistance and awakening in the anti-apartheid movement.

Following the death of Premier Zhou Enlai, spontaneous demonstrations took place in Tiananmen Square, Beijing, mourning Zhou and expressing grievances against the government's policies. While the protests were quelled at the time, they foreshadowed later and more significant protests, including the 1989 Tiananmen Square protests, indicating a growing discontent and a desire for political change among segments of the Chinese population.

Steve Jobs, Steve Wozniak, and Ronald Wayne founded Apple Computer. The establishment of Apple marked the beginning of the personal computer revolution, awakening the public to the transformative potential of computing technology and laying the foundation for the technological advancements of the coming decades.

1988. EARTH DRAGON

President Gorbachev's policies of glasnost (openness) and perestroika (restructuring) initiated a new era of Soviet foreign policy. These reforms aimed at fostering more transparent governance and economic restructuring had a significant impact on Eastern Europe. Gorbachev's willingness to allow greater political and economic freedom in Soviet satellite states, including East Germany, set the stage for political changes in the region.

The Hungarian government, under Prime Minister Miklós Németh, initiated a series of liberalising measures, including dismantling the barbed wire on its border with Austria. This move signalled a departure from strict adherence to the Eastern Bloc's policies and allowed East Germans to escape to the West through Hungary.

The Solidarity movement in Poland, led by Lech Wałęsa, had been challenging the Communist regime for years. By 1988, the Polish government, facing economic difficulties and increasing pressure from the Solidarity movement, began negotiations with opposition leaders. This led to Round Table Talks in 1989 which resulted in the establishment of partially free elections, leading to a shift in power and the eventual dismantling of the Communist system.

2000. METAL DRAGON

The Millennium Summit held by the United Nations in the year 2000 marked a global awakening to the need for collective action to address pressing issues. World leaders adopted the Millennium Development Goals, outlining objectives related to poverty reduction, education, gender equality, and global health. This event emphasised the importance of international cooperation to address global challenges.

Throughout the year 2000, anti-globalization protests gained momentum, with activists rallying against the World Trade Organisation (WTO) and other international institutions. These protests highlighted concerns about the impact of globalisation on workers' rights, environmental sustainability, and social justice, leading to a broader public awakening to the consequences of economic policies.

In October 2000, the United Nations Security Council passed Resolution 1325, recognising the role of women in peacebuilding and conflict resolution. This landmark resolution marked an awakening to the importance of gender perspectives in matters of international peace and security, emphasising the need for women's involvement in decision-making processes.

The first World Social Forum (WSF) took place in Porto Alegre, Brazil, in the year 2000. The WSF provided a platform for civil society organisations and activists to discuss and address issues related to globalisation, social justice, and alternative economic models.

2012. WATER DRAGON

2012 was characterised by many movements, where large groups mobilised in countries across the world to try and enforce change and a fairer society for all. In January 2012, widespread protests erupted in Nigeria in response to the removal of fuel subsidies. The "Occupy Nigeria" movement voiced concerns about the economic impact on citizens, leading to demonstrations and strikes across the country. In Hong Kong activists launched the Occupy Central movement in 2012. The movement protested against income inequality, political corruption, and the perceived influence of Beijing on local affairs. In Russia, protests erupted against Vladimir Putin's return to the presidency. Demonstrators criticised alleged electoral fraud and demanded political reforms. The protests were among the largest in Russia since the 1990s, reflecting public discontent with the political system. In Quebec, Canada, students mobilised against proposed tuition fee increases. The protests, known as the "Maple Spring," involved widespread strikes, demonstrations, and clashes with police, raising broader questions about education policy and youth engagement. Across Europe, particularly in countries facing economic crises, there were widespread protests against austerity measures and economic policies. Greece, Spain, Portugal, and other nations experienced significant demonstrations, with citizens expressing frustration over unemployment, austerity, and perceived social injustices.

WHAT TO EXPECT IN 2024

We cannot predict the future. I cannot tell you what will definitely happen in 2024, but I can give you a sense of what I believe will happen, based on the Wood Dragon's energy, and the themes and situations we have experienced over the last few years. Global events are complex and often unpredictable, but specific ongoing trends and emerging issues are likely to contribute to a sense of awakening in different spheres.

The key themes that I believe will be at the heart of 2024 will be; the environment, technological advancements, social justice and equality, educational reform, and political engagement. In the following pages I offer insights into how I believe the year will unfold against the backdrop of these five trends.

THE ENVIRONMENT

In 2024, the Wood Dragon's impact will be about encouraging everyone to care for the Earth. It will ask us to change how we treat our environment, promoting practices that help the planet stay healthy and full of life. This means things like farming in a way that doesn't harm the Earth, being careful about what we buy, and using technology and social media to spread the word about how important it is to live in balance with the planet.

Leading up to 2024, there has been a huge wave of global activism, especially from young people like Greta Thunberg and Txai Suruí. Inspired by a strong sense of caring for the environment and a commitment to making the world more sustainable, movements like Fridays for Future, Indigenous Movement for Youth, Extinction Rebellion, and Just Stop Oil have gained much support. This is likely to continue and grow in 2024. Young activists will keep raising awareness, organising protests, and pushing leaders and companies to improve. We can expect more people to join these movements, and their voices will become even louder.

This year, there will be a shift in focus, from stopping negative actions from happening to showing how we can make good things occur. While protests are still likely, and larger, they will feel more positive and celebratory. People will be more excited about making positive changes and looking forward to a better future.

A big part of this change is how we all start to feel about the planet, there will be a collective shift of consciousness which will bring about a move towards being more eco-friendly in our daily lives. More people will make conscious choices about what they buy and eat, reducing waste and supporting initiatives like community clean-ups. Cities will become greener and more sustainable, with rooftop gardens and eco-friendly architecture becoming more common.

There will be a growing awareness that although national governments and the international community appear to be making greater strides towards more environmentally friendly initiatives, changes that they are making are less about saving the planet, and more about exercising greater control over their citizens. Whilst individuals will take much more care over the choices that they make, and local community organisations will promote eco-friendly initiatives, people will resist national initiatives as they gain a greater understanding that working with the planet does not have to entail giving up their freedoms.

The switch to renewable energy sources will speed up in 2024. Technology is improving, and more people and companies are realising the importance of clean energy for the planet's future. Fossil fuels will be phased out for sustainable alternatives like solar and wind power.

Businesses are also waking up to the need for sustainability, driven by demand from us the consumer. Companies will adopt eco-friendly practices, as more and more consumers will demand that businesses take responsibility for their environmental impact. Agriculture will focus more on sustainable methods, with small farms using traditional practices thriving as people value where their food comes from.

As the Wood Dragon Year unfolds, its energy aligns with the idea that we must heal the planet. Eco-friendly initiatives and sustainable lifestyles will become more than trends, they will become a collective commitment to respect the Earth and create a legacy of growth, adaptability, and harmony with the natural world.

TECHNOLOGICAL ADVANCEMENTS

Ongoing technological advancements, including artificial intelligence, biotechnology, and increased digitalisation, will likely lead to increased awareness and discussions about these changes' ethical, social, and economic implications as we move through 2024. The energy of the Wood Dragon is a catalyst for change and innovation for the benefit of the many as opposed to the few. We can expect conversations around the role of technology in shaping society to contribute to awakening public consciousness.

While it's always challenging to predict specific technological developments when you are not particularly technologically advanced yourself, (at the time of writing this, I have managed to lock our new coffee machine despite being pretty confident I only pressed the buttons I was shown this morning), I can explore potential themes and trends based on the ongoing trajectory of technological advancements we have seen over the last few years. In 2024, several key areas of technological transformation are likely to shape how we use technology in our lives over the coming year.

Artificial Intelligence has proved to be a game changer in several different fields, revolutionising how we approach problem-solving, streamline processes, and make data-driven decisions, and, in the process, transforming industries such as healthcare, finance, and education. In the arts, artificial intelligence has ushered in a new era of creativity, enabling innovative collaborations between machines and humans, and in the process pushing the boundaries of artistic expression. This has offered unexplored avenues for the generation of music, visual arts, and literature to existing creators, whilst enabling new creators to express their creativity for the very first time. While these have only sometimes been successful, artificial intelligence is expected to become more sophisticated and integrated into various aspects of daily life and business operations as we move through the year. As it takes hold over more and more of our daily tasks, we can expect discussions around its ethical use to gain prominence.

The digital divide remains a concern in many regions. Initiatives to bridge the gap in digital access and literacy, ensuring that all individuals have equal opportunities to participate in the digital age, may become more widespread. 5G technology has the potential to provide improved connectivity in remote or underserved areas, enabling access to information, education and services in regions where traditional infrastructure may be lacking. 5G technology will bring people together, give more people access to services and information and enable faster and more reliable communication. Wood Dragon years tend to be years where there is a levelling up between the haves and the have-nots, and the advancement of 5G technology will lead to transformative changes in the way vast numbers of people can access what they need.

Biotechnology and healthcare technology will likely be at the forefront of advancement as we move through 2024. Wearable health technology and remote patient monitoring will contribute to more efficient and personalised healthcare services, improving patient outcomes. We will likely see a range of innovative technologies being widely rolled out, from smartwatches that track vital signs to wearable sensors monitoring specific health parameters. By enabling continuous, real-time monitoring of patients outside traditional clinical settings, wearable health technology will allow healthcare professionals to gather a wealth of data. This will offer a more comprehensive and dynamic understanding of an individual's health, and facilitate early detection of potential health issues, empowering patients to participate actively in their well-being through self-monitoring. Additionally, remote patient monitoring fosters a shift from reactive to proactive healthcare, as healthcare providers can intervene promptly based on real-time data, potentially preventing complications and reducing hospital readmissions. The integration of wearable health technology into healthcare systems promises to create a more patient-centric and efficient healthcare system, where personalised insights and timely interventions lead to improved overall health outcomes.

As technology evolves, so do cybersecurity threats. In 2024, there may be an increased focus on developing advanced cybersecurity solutions, including AI-driven threat detection, biometric authentication, and secure-by-design principles. The growing awareness of cybersecurity risks may lead to heightened efforts to protect digital assets and privacy.

Innovations addressing environmental challenges like climate change and resource depletion may become more prevalent. This could include advancements in renewable energy, sustainable agriculture technologies, and eco-friendly materials, reflecting a broader awakening to the importance of technology in creating a more sustainable future.

SOCIAL JUSTICE AND EQUALITY

As we move into 2024, the momentum behind the push for inclusivity and diversity is expected to gain even more traction. Evolving cultural norms will likely continue to challenge traditional perspectives, fostering a more inclusive and accepting society. Ongoing discussions around diversity will become even more widespread as individuals and organisations recognise the importance of embracing differences and dismantling barriers. This heightened awareness and commitment to inclusivity will contribute to a cultural awakening, prompting people to reevaluate their own beliefs, biases, and behaviours.

The power of diverse narratives, experiences, and voices is increasingly acknowledged as a driving force for innovation, creativity, and social progress, which aligns perfectly with the energy of the Wood Dragon. In 2024, we may witness an even more concerted effort to create spaces that celebrate diverse perspectives, leading to a society where everyone feels seen, heard, and valued. In countries where diversity and uniqueness are not respected or valued, and those who are seen as different are subject to abuse, intolerance and, in some instances, the threat of death, we may see increasing numbers of protests internally and pressure from the global community at large to enforce change. There is the potential for leaders of these movements to be persecuted, imprisoned or even risk death, and as upsetting and tragic as this is, they will see their sacrifice to be worth it if it makes the lives of those that follow easier and more fulfilled. This collective shift towards embracing diversity has the potential to reshape social and community structures and attitudes.

Efforts to address racial and ethnic inequality are likely to persist. Despite the civil rights act being signed the last time the Wood Dragon appeared, there is still a long way to go before we have true racial and ethnic equality. This year we are likely to see increased efforts to address disparities in education, employment and criminal justice.

Advances in LGBTQ+ rights, and advocacy for inclusivity, are also likely to continue. Efforts to promote equal rights, combat discrimination, and ensure the legal recognition of diverse gender identities and sexual orientations may see progress. There will be a growing acknowledgement of gender and sexual fluidity as well as the destigmatisation of diverse sexual orientations. Legal and policy changes supporting gender diversity may also be part of this evolution and we may well see acts being pushed through parliaments in various countries that protect and recognise gender identities. The push for LGBTQ+ representation in various spheres of public life will also gain traction.

The COVID-19 pandemic highlighted health disparities, and efforts to achieve health equity may intensify in 2024. This could involve addressing unequal access to healthcare, promoting mental health awareness, and confronting social determinants of health that disproportionately affect marginalised communities.

Efforts to promote disability rights and inclusivity may see increased attention. Advocacy for accessible infrastructure, equal employment opportunities, and the dismantling of stigmas surrounding disabilities will contribute to a more inclusive society.

This year, we may witness a notable rise in endeavours that reshape the approach to preserving cultures. Community-led ventures could become instrumental in showcasing cultural heritage, promoting traditional crafts, and creating new and dynamic artistic expressions. Individuals and communities, recognising the value of their cultural roots, may actively engage in projects that preserve and promote their traditions.

During this year, creators such as artists, writers, and filmmakers may explore identity, belonging, and cultural diversity themes within their local communities. Independent artists and self-published writers will likely be rewarded and more widely recognised for their work. Films and books that promote local voices will be more successful than blockbusters and large studio productions focusing on global themes.

Platforms that allow diverse voices and narratives will likely play a crucial role, and social media, digital platforms, and community spaces dedicated to cultural exchange will provide the necessary infrastructure for sharing stories. The Year of the Wood Dragon will ensure those who have played a large part in maintaining the cultural legacy are celebrated.

EDUCATIONAL REFORMS

Ongoing educational changes, driven by technology, may lead to re-evaluating traditional education systems. Conversations about accessibility, lifelong learning, and the role of education in shaping future societies could contribute to an educational awakening in the year of the Wood Dragon.

The integration of technology in education is expected to accelerate in 2024. Virtual and augmented reality, artificial intelligence, and interactive digital platforms may become integral to the learning experience. This transformation could lead to more personalised and adaptive learning environments, catering much more to diverse learning styles and individual needs. As more recognition is given to children learning in different ways, and with it an understanding that the approach to traditional schooling can disengage some children, we will likely see attendance at schools increase as they adapt to new ways of learning.

The lessons learned from the COVID-19 pandemic will continue to shape educational practices. Remote and blended learning models, combining in-person and online elements, will likely become more widespread. Educational institutions may develop flexible and resilient approaches to ensure continuity in learning, even in the face of unforeseen disruptions.

Recognising the need for continuous skill development throughout people's lives will drive the expansion of lifelong learning initiatives. Educational institutions, employers, and governments will collaborate to provide accessible and flexible learning opportunities for individuals to upskill and reskill. There will be a greater focus on transitioning from school to work.

Collaborations between educational institutions and communities, as well as partnerships with industries, may become more prevalent. These partnerships could lead to co-creating educational programs that align with real-world needs and provide students with practical experiences. Apprenticeships, internships, and mentorship programs may be integrated into educational pathways.

The theme of education transformation includes a commitment to inclusivity and diversity. Efforts to create inclusive learning environments that accommodate students of diverse backgrounds, abilities, and learning preferences may be at the forefront. Inclusive education practices may involve curriculum adjustments, accessible learning materials, and support for students with diverse needs. Open educational resources and open-access materials may become more widespread, promoting greater accessibility to educational content. This shift could contribute to reducing barriers to education and fostering a culture of knowledge-sharing and collaboration.

Recognising the importance of social-emotional skills, education transformation in 2024 may prioritise the development of emotional intelligence, resilience, and interpersonal skills. Social-emotional learning programs may be integrated into the curriculum to support students' well-being and prepare them for the social complexities of the future.

This transformation of education will involve a parallel focus on teachers' professional development. Teachers may engage in ongoing training to adapt to new technologies, teaching methods, and evolving educational theories. Professional development opportunities may be designed to empower educators as facilitators of student-centred learning experiences.

POLITICAL ENGAGEMENT

In 2024, the theme of political awakening is likely to involve various developments that show people are paying more attention to politics, getting involved in their communities, and demanding open and accountable leaders. People worldwide will push for changes in elections to ensure transparency and that every vote counts. In some places where leaders hold too much power, there might be large protests calling for fair elections and changes to the rules.

Young people are expected to become more politically active, leading movements to bring about political changes. In areas where there are elections, there will likely be a focus on getting more young people into influential positions in the government. Technology and social media will play a big part in this, as young activists use online platforms to make their voices heard and push for a more youth-influenced government.

Political awakening also means paying attention to human rights issues. Activists and groups will stress how crucial it is to protect the rights of all people, especially those who are often left out or mistreated. Movements might call for the release of people who were imprisoned for political reasons, an end to government-sponsored oppression, and the promotion of the human rights that everyone should have. This political awareness will not just be about national politics, but will also happen within local communities. Grassroots movements may push for more say in local decision-making, fair budgeting that involves the community, and changes to local policies. Having leaders who listen and are accountable to their communities will become even more important.

The dynamics of political movements and counter-movements will likely continue shaping the political landscapes of different nations. Over the last few years many countries have elected leaders who are charismatic and appeal to a broad base of people, and this year they may face increased scrutiny as the substance of their messages comes under question. There will be a growing demand for transparency and adherence to democratic norms as societies become more aware of the potential risks associated with populist governments.

Concurrently, counter-movements that advocate for more inclusive and progressive governance are gaining momentum. These movements focus on issues like diversity, social justice, and equal representation, aiming to counter the perceived exclusivity and polarisation of populist ideologies. The clash between these opposing political forces is poised to influence political discourse and policy decisions in various regions.

Discussions revolving around nationalism, globalism, and the role of populism in shaping political ideologies are expected to remain central. Nationalism, championed by populist leaders, may face challenges from globalists who stress interconnectedness, cooperation, and addressing transnational issues collaboratively. This tension is not limited to domestic policies, it will also extend to international relations and diplomacy.

The influence of populism on political ideologies may prompt a re-evaluation of traditional political distinctions. The impact of populist narratives on economic policies, immigration, and social welfare could redefine political ideologies, blurring the lines between conventional left-right categories. This evolution in political thought may require a reassessment of political strategies and alliances in response to a more complex and dynamic landscape.

12 PREDICTIONS FOR 2024

1. New youth led movements will form, and there will be mergers between some existing protest groups. Whilst there will still be protests, as the year progresses we are likely to see increased examples of civil disobedience to create change. Increasingly people who have never taken part in protests before will be involved as the Wood Dragon brings with it an energy that allows people to realise that the world cannot continue on its current trajectory.

2. More cities and towns will implement cleaner air measures, offering greater incentives to people to use greener modes of transportation and in the process penalising those who use more traditional methods of transport. Car drivers will feel aggrieved at the direction local governments are taking, and their could be protests and unrest in major urban areas.

3. As the world transitions towards cleaner energy sources, the regions that once dominated the supply of fossil fuels may find their influence diminishing as the focus shifts towards sustainable and eco-friendly energy solutions. Expect Australia and the African continent to be the winners, whilst the Middle East and South American countries lose out.

4. As artificial intelligence becomes an ever-increasing part of our lives, there will be a potential showdown between computer and human-generated content. This clash sparks questions about each side's role and how it will affect what we read, watch, and listen to. There will be a general lack of trust in the information we are being fed, leading people to seek out new ways of communication.

5. 5G technology will continue to rollout across regions, giving access to the internet to greater numbers of people across the globe this year. With this comes a growing awareness of the disparity in freedoms that people in different parts of the world enjoy, and their may well be uprisings in countries who's leaders exert more control over people's daily lives. Expect the youth in these countries to be the force behind driving change.

6. There will be significant shifts in healthcare this year, as technology will provide more data on patient health and allows patient care to be provided away from hospital settings. With this comes a growing concern that governments are able to access and control individuals in a way that they never have before, and many people will turn to alternative treatments as a way to feel more in control of their own bodies.

7. The focus on equality will very much be on LGBTQ+ rights this year, with more countries decriminalising same sex intimacy, and legalising same sex marriage. This will, globally, lead to those people in countries and regions where this is still supressed gaining the confidence to have a voice. There will be conflict and a battle between those who want the freedom to be themselves, and the same rights as others, and those who want to maintain the status quo.

8. Self-published books, small independent films, and community-produced podcasts will be the winners in the arts, as people turn away from traditional, and large company produced material. There are likely to be protests against at least one major studio, or media organisation as it is discovered that they have been trying to control the narrative. As smaller, self-produced material gain traction, governments across the world may try to censor or silence smaller voices in the media, including governments which outwardly appear to encourage disparate views.

9. As the world becomes every increasingly open, their will be an increased desire within communities to protect their cultural heritage. There will be calls for local languages to be taught in schools and promoted within businesses, and regions will demand ever more devolved powers from national governments.

10. There will continue to be a shift in the way children are taught in schools, and an ever increasing concern that traditional teaching methods are not preparing children for life once they leave school. There will be greater calls for less focus on academic achievement. Concerns in teaching methods will lead to more people home-schooling than ever before, and many local community organisations will form to support parents who are home-schooling.

11. Many elections are happening worldwide in 2024, and the choices people are faced with may well lead to mass protests. Leaders with bold and sometimes extreme ideas are in the ascendency, which leads to division, and many people will feel that it is not a case of who they want to win but who they don't. This means that many people will question if current electoral systems work, and protest for a new type of democracy. In many countries smaller parties, or independent politicians will do well.

12. As people's confidence in governments to address their fundamental needs diminishes, a trend will emerge in forming new community groups and charities. Individuals will create grassroots organisations driven by a shared commitment to managing healthcare, education, housing, and social welfare at the community level. This shift towards localised, community-driven efforts reflects a growing belief in individuals' power to impact the well-being of their fellow community members directly.

2024. WHAT IT MEANS FOR US

As we have seen, the year of the Wood Dragon will shift the collective perspective and impact all our lives. Because each Chinese zodiac sign embodies unique characteristics and traits, these changes will differ for each of us. Let us look at what this fresh global perspective could mean, and identify the potential opportunities, challenges, and transformative energies ahead. Whether you are a resourceful Rat, a diligent Ox, a charismatic Dragon, or any of the other nine animal signs, read on to see how you can make the most of the year before you.

THE RAT

As the rat transitions into the Year of the Wood Dragon, you can do so with a high degree of optimism and confidence. Wood Dragons are innovative, visionary leaders, and the quick-witted, resourceful rat is well-placed to make the most of any opportunities that the wood dragon year may throw up. Entering this year, you may find yourself inspired to set ambitious goals that you strive to achieve with enthusiasm and motivation.

Rats are charming and friendly, and these traits combine with the Wood Dragon's magnetic energy to create a potent social influence. Networking and building strong connections with others can open doors for you to exciting opportunities, both personally and professionally. As the world mobilises to make the planet a better place, you are likely to be at the forefront of movements to make immediate changes for the good of all. If one route is blocked, you can quickly find another that you can lead people down to get what you and they want. A rat can rarely be thwarted when someone tries to stop them, and in the wood dragon year, it is even more unlikely that you will be able to be controlled. You can be sure that where there is a will the rat will find a way.

Positives

- You may find yourself increasingly in the right place at the right time. This can lead to greater exposure and recognition for your unique talents and skills.
- Hidden talents may come to the fore, leading to breakthroughs in various aspects of your life that you hadn't necessarily considered before.
- When obstacles appear in your path, you will have the support and encouragement of your friends to overcome them.

Negatives

- The surge of positive energy in the universe this year, may also lead others to take advantage of situations, providing you with increased competition and added pressure to make the most of opportunities. Do not let this cause you stress. Wood Dragon energy is very potent and there will be plenty to go around.

THE OX

The year of the wood dragon may be challenging for those of you born in the year of the ox. That is not to say that the year will be unlucky or problematic, just that you may feel that change is happening too quickly and you are losing control of your life and your place within it. Ox are known for approaching tasks methodically and slowly. When you do not think you have the time to put a plan together to control a situation, you may struggle to make sense of the changes around you, leading to feelings of disquiet and uncertainty.

If Ox are going to make the most of the opportunities that will arise in the year of the Wood Dragon, then you would benefit from adopting a more flexible and adaptable mindset. Technological changes especially are going to happen whether you embrace them or not. You are known for your strength and determination and will be diligent and hardworking when you set your mind to something, so balancing these traits with adaptability can lead you to navigate through the innovative changes the year will bring and turn challenges into opportunities smoothly. After all, wood dragon years can be filled with abundance for those prepared to make the most of the opportunities. The Ox is one of the most hardworking signs in the zodiac, and it would be a shame if you missed out on all the year can offer because you were over-cautious, whilst others were more prepared to take a risk.

Positives

- The combination of hard work and auspicious energy may lead to financial bonuses or promotions at work.
- Important relationships with friends and family may strengthen. Any new relationships that you form are likely to be strong and lasting.

Negatives

- The year may bring increased workloads and additional responsibilities which take a toll on your health and well-being.
- The cautious and reserved nature of the ox may clash with the strong assertive energy of the dragon, leading to misunderstandings in conversations and situations. You may struggle to make sense of a lot of what is happening and what you are being told and find comfort in the status quo.

THE TIGER

At first glance, the tiger and the wood dragon share many traits and qualities, so you would assume that those born in the year of the tiger would have a good year in the year of the wood dragon. But often in life it is those who are opposites who are attracted to each other, and in the tiger and the dragon relationship this year it is more a case of familiarity breeding contempt. The tiger and the dragon are too similar. In a year that promises many boundless opportunities and innovative changes, the tiger and the dragon are likely to compete with each other to get the bigger share of the spoils.

That is not to say that those born in the year of the tiger are predicted to have a bad year. Just that you need to be mindful how you use your courage, enthusiasm and dynamic energy to take yourself forward without trying to trample on anyone else. The year can be favourable for the tigers if you curb your desire to win at all costs and allow yourself instead to go with the flow. To embrace change, even if you are not the ones who forced it, to recognise that you can take others with you, even if you do not lead.

Where tigers may struggle this year is in their unpredictability. When things do not go your way, you can give in and refuse to participate in what is happening. If a tiger does not like or agree with the changes that occur this year, you may decide to sit them out, which could be a mistake because you could find yourself left behind, and end the year in a worse place than when you entered it.

Positives

- You may experience a surge of opportunities to advance your career or business.
- You may be inspired to explore your artistic side and in the process discover hidden talents that you can use.

Negatives

- Watch out for making impulsive choices. They may work out for you, but this will be down to luck not good judgement, and it would be a mistake to repeat them, expecting the same good fortune to strike twice.

- You may have a tendency to take risks, and make decisions based on gut feelings rather than detailed analysis of the facts.

THE RABBIT

The year of the wood dragon is a year where the rabbit's natural diplomatic and harmonious nature may be called upon repeatedly. In a year where, across the world, many people will be moved to create change for the good of the planet, there will equally be those who want to stop them, to maintain the status quo, to ensure that the values that have stood the world in good stead over the years remain. Helping bring those two factions together will require massive degrees of tact and diplomacy and the skills of the rabbit will be called upon time and time again to try and bridge what may seem to be a great divide.

What this may mean for the rabbit is that you may be put under more stress than you are comfortable with. Rabbits are compassionate and love to nurture and care for people, but those who care for others also need to care for themselves. If the rabbit is to have a positive and productive year, where you get what you want from the year, as well as helping others get what they want, then you should prioritise your health and wellbeing and not be afraid to ask for support yourself. Weakness is not in accepting you need help, but in thinking you are too strong to need it.

Positives

- Your natural ability to empathise and understand others perspectives will ensure you are a popular friend this year.
- This is a year where you can embark on a journey of self-discovery. Pursue hobbies and interests that bring you joy. Make sure you prioritise yourself for once, instead of focusing on the needs of others. You deserve it.

Negatives

- You may have difficulty asserting boundaries and saying no. Guard against people taking advantage of your good nature.
- Do not allow yourself to become overwhelmed by the demands of others. You cannot support other people if you are not looking after your own health and wellbeing.

THE DRAGON

It's your year, dragon, and although the year of the wood dragon only comes around every 60 years, all dragons should and can make the most of this year. As a dragon you are known for your ambition and enthusiasm, and all dragons can tap into this energy to make this year their best year yet. Let that inspiration surge and explore creative endeavours in business or the arts. The more innovative the idea, and the more passion you put into it, the more successful you are likely to be.

The dragon is a natural leader, and this year, as the world wakes to a new dawn, is a year for people to take the lead. The energy of the wood dragon will call on all leaders to showcase their skills and contribute to their communities. This is a year where you can make a difference in your life and the lives of all the people you touch. To add caution, though, you must balance ambition with practicality. People will look to you to take the lead to improve their lives, and with that comes the responsibility to not over-promise what you can't deliver.

Positives

- You are likely to find yourself radiating with confidence and attracting positive attention from others. This is a year for expressing yourself and letting the authentic you shine.

- This is a fortunate and abundant year for you, dragon. Luck is likely to be on your side, so make the most of anything that seems to be going well for you without much effort on your part. Ride that wave.

- You are likely to be lucky in love, so if you are single and looking for a mate, or want to rekindle romance, this is the year to put yourself out there and let others know what you want.

Negatives

- Do not let yourself become over confident as this has the potential to come across as arrogance. Let your spirit soar, but keep your feet on the ground.

THE SNAKE

The year of the wood dragon is likely to be a good year for snakes, as snakes are in their element when presented with a new idea and an opportunity for growth. Your wise, detail-orientated minds are perfect for taking an idea and coming up with a plan of action which you can implement for your benefit, and the benefit of those around you. As the year of the wood dragon will be a year of change, those born in the year of the snake will benefit from setting clear objectives and taking a calculated approach to turn ideas into a plan and an outcome. Trusting your instincts and making informed decisions will be critical to your success.

Dragon years can be filled with good fortune and abundance, and the wood dragon year will be no different, although abundance will be less focused on material wealth and more on planetary health. You may experience stability and growth in your financial and business affairs. You can do good work supporting visionaries who have an idea but cannot apply it practically to make it work. Snakes can add a dose of realism and a pinch of pragmatism to turn a dream into something tangible, and so you should look out for others who may need your planning and decision-making skills. This could be a year for snakes to build new alliances in both personal and professional circles.

Positives

- Trust your instincts and don't question why. This year they will rarely be wrong.

- Your magnetic presence and natural charm are heightened this year. You have the ability to influence people and make an impact on the world, so take advantage of it, and use your power for good.

- No problem is insurmountable this year. No matter what obstacles are strewn in your path, with your wisdom you will be able to navigate through them with ease.

Negatives

- With your magnetic personality you have the ability to manipulate people to do what you want them to do. Be careful, snake, because just as you can use your power for good, there is also another way in which it can be used.

THE HORSE

Horses are known for their boundless energy and sense of adventure. At first glance, the year of the wood dragon, which brings a fresh perspective and significant change, suggests that those born under the year of the horse will thrive this year. However, whilst there are opportunities to follow, and new possibilities to explore, the year may be scattered with frustrations and conflict as things may go differently than you expected.

For the horse, the year of the wood dragon is ultimately one in which you may feel that you have not achieved all you thought was possible. You have not been able to meet your full potential or have the desired impact on the world that you hoped you would. It is unlikely that the year will be bad, just not as good as you hoped. It is as though a year that has promised so much delivered so little. Unrealistic expectations, changes that happened slowly, and unforeseen obstacles will likely prey on your mind and surround you with negativity. You could feel the year is holding on tight to your reins, and not giving you the freedom you let your dreams run free.

Positives

- You are a free spirit and have a sense of fun and adventure. The year could be tough for you, but stay positive and you can handle whatever the year throws your way.

Negatives

- You may find yourself getting restless and distracted. The year is not going to be the easiest ride of your life, but don't let that take you off course. Stay focused and things will work out for you.
- You may feel the need to constantly prove yourself as you are likely to encounter competition in your career or business. Do not put so much pressure on yourself that you can't handle it.

THE GOAT

Goats are known for their artistic and creative inclinations, and in the year of the wood dragon, this creative energy may be heightened. If you were born in the year of the goat, you will likely find the inspiration to take a new hobby or creative pursuit and be drawn to activities that allow you to express yourself and your talents in unique and exciting ways.

The wood dragon's harmonious and sociable energy aligns well with the goat's gentle and pleasant nature, and the year may bring opportunities to enhance relationships with friends and those who share common interests. Communication and collaboration may lead you to find connections with like-minded people and form firm bonds of friendship. These relationships can have a positive contribution to the lives not only of those who share them but also of the broader community.

Whether building connections for pleasure or fostering those relationships for good in the community, the year of the wood dragon will likely bring great satisfaction to the goat, and you will probably end the year feeling a sense of fulfilment and achievement.

Positives

- Artistic and creative pursuits abound this year, so take advantage of the multitude of opportunities and find a new hobby or creative endeavour that you want to try, and give it a go.
- You are likely to find yourself more in tune with your spiritual side. Follow your inner guidance which will lead you on a journey of personal growth, self-discovery and give you a greater sense of peace and fulfilment in your life.

Negatives

- You may find yourself overwhelmed by the abundance of opportunities and unsure which path to take, leading you to take none and miss out on what should rightfully be yours.
- Be on your guard against people taking advantage of your good nature. Set boundaries and be discerning with who to get close to this year.

THE MONKEY

After the dragon, the monkey is probably the zodiac animal sign that is most likely to have an excellent year. Monkeys are known for their quick thinking and adaptability, and these traits may prove particularly valuable in the year of the wood dragon. As the wood dragon's influence encourages innovation and growth, you may find yourself drawn to new and creative ventures in your personal or professional life. This is a favourable time for you to explore unique ideas and take calculated risks to increase your influence and standing in the world.

The dynamic energy of the wood dragon aligns well with your communicative nature. This period may enhance the communication skills of those born in the year of the monkey, allowing you to express ideas more effectively and build positive connections. Monkeys are not always natural leaders, but your sense of fun and mischief naturally draws people to you, and you are adept at persuading others to your point of view. Where a group of people is trying to enforce change for good, you can be sure there will be a monkey trying to draw others into the cause. As fundraisers or cheerleaders, monkeys can mobilise others and, even in the darkest of times, can bring some much needed cheer to lift the spirits to live and fight another day.

Positives

- With your intelligence and adaptability you can turn your hands to most things. The year will throw up lots of new opportunities for you to exploit to achieve everything you desire.
- You thrive when circumstances change, and your quick wit and easy charm will help you navigate the changing year with ease.
- New connections are likely to be charmed by you, which will lead to doors being opened to lots of bright new possibilities. Make the most of them.

Negatives

- With so many opportunities to take advantage of, you may easily become distracted by something new and risk starting lots of exciting activities but never seeing them through.

THE ROOSTER

The year of the wood dragon will be a mixed year for the roosters among you. Your confident and expressive nature will be enhanced, and there will be many opportunities for you to highlight your talents to others, present yourself with confidence and grab hold of the many opportunities that the wood dragon puts in your path. Some of these may be unexpected, and as the year progresses, you may participate in activities or follow goals that you hadn't even thought of at the beginning of the year. The year will throw up many changes you are unlikely to be phased by; when something happens and you think you can benefit from it, you will be in there whether you can do it or not.

And that is when the year may throw up some challenges for you. There is a fine line between taking advantage of a situation where you have the skills and knowledge to navigate it, and trying to take advantage of a situation hoping blind faith will see you through. You will not always find yourself on the right side of the line, rooster, and if you try and bite off more than you can chew, rather than take advantage of a situation, you may find the situation takes advantage of you. Fortune does not always favour the brave, and whilst the year has endless possibilities, the universe rewards those who most deserve it.

Positives

- Opportunities may arise to take the lead in new projects or initiatives. If you want to advance in your career, this year could throw up the possibility of promotion.
- Checking the small print of contracts, or going over the fine details of plans, could pay dividends this year, as you may discover opportunities in areas which others have missed.

Negatives

- You have a tendency to strive for perfection, but the fresh energy of the wood dragon means this year is a work in progress. Trying to get everything right in a year where actions are sometimes not thought through can cause you unnecessary angst.
- Try not to be overly critical of those who are trying to make a difference, but haven't put together a plan. The world changes fast, and you sometimes have to go with the flow.

THE DOG

Dogs are known for their loyalty and strong sense of teamwork, and the year of the wood dragon will make the poor dog feel a little unsettled. Not because the dog doesn't like change, because you can accept that change is part of life, but because change can often throw up chaos and conflict. Even when it is done with the best of intentions and to try to make the world a better place.

Dogs do not like to feel that people are not getting along with each other, and although many people will be working together to achieve a common goal, there will be others who want things to stay as they are, or for the changes to go in a different direction. This will pit people against each other, and caught in the middle, the dog will not know which way to turn. The dog wants everyone to get along, and if that means things staying as they are and everyone muddling through, it will feel better than one person winning if someone else loses.

Positives

* In a year of change there is always uncertainty, and you can always be relied upon to offer support when needed. Relationships formed this year are likely to last.

Negatives

* If you agree with the changes that are happening around you, you are happy to go with the flow, but if you don't beware. Your stubbornness and inflexibility to see another point of view may put you into conflict with people this year.
* Your natural protectiveness of those you love, may lead you to be suspicious of the motives of those who want to get close. You may need to learn to trust more, for this does not always mean you have to let down your guard.

- The reluctance to get involved may put you on the sidelines of events, and those born in the year of the dog may miss out on some opportunities that come your way.

THE BOAR

Boars are known for their kindness and cooperative nature and will be in high demand as the wood dragon breathes winds of change through the year. These qualities, coupled with your well-grounded attitude, will mean you will find many opportunities to collaborate, build strong alliances, and foster positive relationships. When communication gets hot-tempered, ideas run riot, and actions look like they will spiral out of control, you will be there, with a pragmatic view, soothing words, and a sense of calm to highlight how chaos does not always have to accompany significant change.

On a personal level, the boar will find the year brings mixed blessings. As growth and expansion seem likely, those born in the year of the boar may want to get involved in everything that is happening. To, if you pardon the expression, put your nose in every trough. Your pragmatic nature, though, will quickly help you identify whether the opportunity is worth pursuing or if it offers too little return for too much effort. Pulling away may mean you see others getting ahead, but never fear. A year has many days, and you don't have to make the most of every one.

Positives

- You are likely to find yourself more inclined to give back to the community this year. Your acts of kindness can have a positive impact on others and create a sense of harmony and goodwill.
- Your ability to bounce back from setbacks and overcome obstacles will stand you in good stead this year, even if things do not always work out as planned. Not every rainbow leads to a pot of gold.

Negatives

- With the year throwing up an almost limitless list of possibilities, you may try to do too much and tire yourself out.
- When people get together to fight for a cause there are always two sides, and both sides invariably disagree. Whichever side you are on, you are likely to come across criticism. Try not to take it personally, for if you dwell on it too long, you may suffer unnecessarily.

FENG SHUI TIPS FOR THE YEAR OF THE WOOD DRAGON

As we enter the year of the wood dragon we can look for ways to align the energy in our environment with our internal energies to maximise the opportunities that the year will bring. Feng Shui, literally translated as wind and water, brings balance between these two opposite forces to create harmony in our environment thereby ensuring our lives are infused with positivity and abundance. Let us finish this book, by identifying what each of us can do to make the most of the year ahead.

In Feng Shui, different sectors of our living and working space are associated with specific aspects of our life. In the year of the wood dragon, the east and south-east areas are the most important, as it is in these two directions that the wood dragon resides. These two areas support new beginnings, abundance, family, close personal and work relationships, and growth. Activate the energy in these two areas by displaying healthy plants with lush green foliage to amplify the wood element. The presence of living plants serves as a visual reminder of the new opportunities that the year will bring and help to symbolise growth, renewal, and rebirth. When displaying plants in these sectors ensure that they are potted in square or rectangular wooden pots and planters, as these will further strengthen the wood element in these areas of your home.

Wooden elements are highly favourable in these sectors during the year of the wood dragon. If you do not have a huge amount of wooden furniture in this area, especially if in your own home this area covers the kitchen or bathroom, you should consider introducing wooden elements in the form of decorations, or art pieces. This can include items crafted from natural wood, such as bamboo or teak, or faux wood. Photograph frames, wooden animal ornaments, small bowls or chests can work very well if you do not have a lot of space. If it is difficult to incorporate wooden elements, then display pictures or photographs of trees, plants or flowers. The goal is to create an environment that resonates with the energy of the wood dragon. Be mindful of the balance within these sectors, ensuring that the presence of the wood element is harmonious and not overwhelming.

Dragons symbolise strength, luck, and prosperity in Chinese culture, and of course in the year of the wood dragon, we should try and integrate dragon symbols into our décor to invite auspicious energy. This can be in dragon figurines, artwork, or even textiles with dragon motifs. For those seeking a more subtle approach, you might choose dragon-themed accessories like throw pillows, rugs, or wall art. These accents serve as constant reminders of the positive attributes dragons bring, fostering a sense of courage, resilience, and the capacity to soar to new heights. Place these items in the east or south-east area, or alternatively where you spend most of your time like the living room, or a home office.

Clearing clutter is a fundamental Feng Shui practice. Decluttering your space allows for the free flow of energy and eliminates obstacles that may hinder progress. At the time of the new year, welcome the wood dragon by refreshing your living or working areas with a thorough cleaning, and consider rearranging furniture to facilitate the smooth flow of energy throughout your home.

As you declutter, pay special attention to areas associated with the wood element, the east and southeast sectors. Clearing these spaces of unnecessary items allows for the unobstructed flow of wood energy, promoting personal growth and new beginnings. As you rearrange furniture or decorative elements, keep in mind the principles of Feng Shui. Ensure that pathways are obvious, allowing energy to circulate freely. Consider the placement of mirrors strategically, as they can be used to expand and enhance the energy in a room.

Once the decluttering process is complete, consider a comprehensive cleaning to refresh the energy in your space. Dust and clean surfaces, open windows to invite fresh air, and perhaps incorporate natural scents, such as essential oils or fragrant plants, to revitalise the atmosphere. Woody scents like sandalwood, palo santo or sage are especially good to burn this year.

Decluttering and refreshing your space is both a physical endeavour and a symbolic one. It signifies a commitment to letting go of the old and making space for the new. As you enter the year of the wood dragon with a decluttered and refreshed environment, you set the stage for a year filled with positive energy, growth, and the unfolding of new possibilities. This intentional cleansing and renewal becomes a powerful catalyst for aligning your surroundings with the auspicious energies of the year, creating a foundation for success and well-being.

FINAL THOUGHTS

As we enter the year of awakening, we find ourselves standing on the threshold of a new, fairer, more equitable era. The wood dragon will herald the start of a period of growth and renewal, where it is not what we have but what we can give that will be most important. It is a year where many will discover a new-found strength within themselves to make changes in their own lives and the lives of others. Connections will be created and built through shared values, objectives and experiences. We can all look forward to a future of hope and new beginnings, whatever zodiac sign we are and whatever stage of life we are at. The wood dragon will breathe new life into all of our souls.

CHINESE NEW YEAR DATES

Year	Chinese New Year	Zodiac Animal
1930	30th January	Metal Horse
1931	17th February	Metal Goat
1932	6th February	Water Monkey
1933	26th January	Water Rooster
1934	14th February	Wood Dog
1935	4th February	Wood Boar
1936	24th January	Fire Rat
1937	11th February	Fire Ox
1938	31st January	Earth Tiger
1939	19th February	Earth Rabbit
1940	8th February	Metal Dragon
1941	27th January	Metal Snake
1942	15th February	Water Horse
1943	4th February	Water Goat
1944	25th January	Wood Monkey
1945	13th February	Wood Rooster
1946	1st February	Fire Dog
1947	22nd January	Fire Boar

1948	10th February	Earth Rat
1949	29th January	Earth Ox
1950	17th February	Metal Tiger
1951	6th February	Metal Rabbit
1952	27th January	Water Dragon
1953	14th February	Water Snake
1954	3rd February	Wood Horse
1955	24th January	Wood Goat
1956	12th February	Fire Monkey
1957	31st January	Fire Rooster
1958	18th February	Earth Dog
1959	8th February	Earth Boar
1960	28th January	Metal Rat
1961	15th February	Metal Ox
1962	5th February	Water Tiger
1963	25th January	Water Rabbit
1964	13th February	Wood Dragon
1965	2nd February	Wood Snake
1966	21st January	Fire Horse
1967	9th February	Fire Goat
1968	30th January	Earth Monkey
1969	17th February	Earth Rooster
1970	6th February	Metal Dog
1971	27th January	Metal Boar
1972	15th February	Water Rat
1973	3rd February	Water Ox

1974	23rd January	Wood Tiger
1975	11th February	Wood Rabbit
1976	31st January	Fire Dragon
1977	18th February	Fire Snake
1978	7th February	Earth Horse
1979	28th January	Earth Goat
1980	16th February	Metal Monkey
1981	5th February	Metal Rooster
1982	25th January	Water Dog
1983	13th February	Water Boar
1984	2nd February	Wood Rat
1985	20th February	Wood Ox
1986	9th February	Fire Tiger
1987	29th January	Fire Rabbit
1988	17th February	Earth Dragon
1989	6th February	Earth Snake
1990	27th January	Metal Horse
1991	15th February	Metal Goat
1992	4th February	Water Monkey
1993	23rd January	Water Rooster
1994	10th February	Wood Dog
1995	31st January	Wood Boar
1996	19th February	Fire Rat
1997	7th February	Fire Ox
1998	28th January	Earth Tiger
1999	16th February	Earth Rabbit

2000	5th February	Metal Dragon
2001	24th January	Metal Snake
2002	12th February	Water Horse
2003	1st February	Water Goat
2004	22nd January	Wood Monkey
2005	9th February	Wood Rooster
2006	29th January	Fire Dog
2007	18th February	Fire Boar
2008	7th February	Earth Rat
2009	26th January	Earth Ox
2010	14th February	Metal Tiger
2011	3rd February	Metal Rabbit
2012	23rd January	Water Dragon
2013	10th February	Water Snake
2014	31st January	Wood Horse
2015	19th February	Wood Goat
2016	8th February	Fire Monkey
2017	28th January	Fire Rooster
2018	16th February	Earth Dog
2019	5th February	Earth Boar
2020	25th January	Metal Rat
2021	12th February	Metal Ox
2022	1st February	Water Tiger
2023	22nd January	Water Rabbit
2024	10th February	Wood Dragon

ABOUT THE AUTHOR

Andrew Laycock is a spiritual writer, teacher and coach. His books are available in paperback and eBook format.

Andrew lives in Dorset, on the south coast of the UK. He can often be found at mind, body, spirit events across the UK. He travels extensively and is happy to talk about his work at workshops or events.

To contact Andrew email: Andrew@resetandrevive.com.

Website: www.resetandrevive.com

Printed in Great Britain
by Amazon

36457881R00040